UNRAVELING FEELINGS TOWARDS LOVE:

A Pregnant Mama's Daily Thoughts

SET IN SOUL

THIS JOURNAL BELONGS TO

DEDICATED TO THE LOVE
GROWING WITHIN ME. ALLOW
ME TO LOVE YOU.

TABLE OF CONTENTS

HOW TO USE THIS JOURNAL

Are you ready to be a mom? Are you happy? Are you nervous? Do you feel ready? Your to-do list is probably driving you crazy. So much to think about before your baby is born, but more importantly, you may feel like you have so much you want to get done before he or she arrives. Learning that you will be a mom for the first time or again brings various emotions. It can be viewed as a miracle to some who feel ready, have been trying to conceive, or just welcome the surprise. To others, learning that you are pregnant may feel life-threatening depending on where you are in your life and what you want for yourself. While we believe babies are a blessing, we know that everyone is at a different stage in their life when they find out they are pregnant.

As you begin to realize that this miracle is really happening, you may become so engrossed with your daily thoughts and actions of preparing to be a mother that it becomes easy to forget about you. So can you do this? We believe you can, but you must also be able to take care of you. You may be thinking you're too young, too old, things aren't right, or you don't have the support. Some of your thoughts may even scare you, so you keep them to yourself. On the flip side, you may just be so happy and so ready and want to express yourself to remember this time in your life. These thoughts of yours are important and they do matter. Keeping a journal of your thoughts and feelings as you prepare to become a mom will not only help you to unleash love and joy, but also help you express beliefs you may feel that you cannot currently say or explain to others. Releasing is a form of healing as well as an expression of love towards yourself. During this transition in your life, you are not to forget about you. There is a way to prepare for motherhood while still staying connected to who you are as well as your baby. This time in your life is to be loved, celebrated and most importantly connected to who you are and who you are becoming.

This journal is broken up into two daily prompt sections with the first section taking you through the first four months of your pregnancy and the second section taking you through the following two months of your pregnancy (which in total covers six months of your pregnancy). These sections move you from unraveling your feelings to standing in your peace and celebrating. Before each section, there is a section called 'Mommy To Be Thoughts' where you will answer questions that get to the core of how you are feeling and what you need. We recommend using this journal daily. This journal is designed to help you feel at peace in this current season in your life as well as be a constant reminder that YOU are important in this process of becoming a mother. This is your time to gain clarity, understanding, and to feel love from God who is within you. Fill out this journal every night to reflect on your day. Fall in love with the quotes that are there to assure you of the blessing that is within you. It doesn't matter how your baby was conceived, what your support system looks like, etc. We believe you have been chosen to be on this path for a reason, and whatever that reason is …. you are blessed. So let's start unraveling.

MOMMY WORDS AND MEANINGS

MIRACLE - a welcoming and surprising event by the power of God

LOVE - the act of giving and caring for someone else unconditionally and having someone's best interest and well-being as a priority in your life

UNEXPECTED - surprising, unseen and not expected as something to happen

TRYING - an attempt or effort to achieve

BLESSING - God's favor and protection

CHOSEN - having been picked out or selected as the best or most appropriate

PARENT - to be or act as a mother or father

MY FIRST, MY LAST, AND EVERYTHING IN-BETWEEN

MY FIRST, MY LAST, AND EVERYTHING IN-BETWEEN

My Last Period Cycle Started On:

Early Pregnancy Symptoms I Started To Experience:

The Day I Found Out That I Was Pregnant:

The Day I Told My Partner That We Are Expecting:

My First Day Of Morning Sickness Was:

MY FIRST, MY LAST, AND EVERYTHING IN-BETWEEN

My First Doctor's Appointment Concerning You:

My First Ultrasound Regarding You:

Special Vitamins I Am Taking For Us:

The First Time I Heard Your Heartbeat:

The Day I Found Out Your Gender:

MY FIRST, MY LAST, AND EVERYTHING IN-BETWEEN

The Day I Chose Your First Name:

The Day I Chose Your Middle Name:

My First Pregnancy Photo Was Taken:

The First Time I Went Shopping For You:

My Last Glass Of Wine Was:

MY FIRST, MY LAST, AND EVERYTHING IN-BETWEEN

My First Odd Craving:

I Now Crave:

The Day I Noticed I Could No Longer Fit Into My Favorite Pair Of Jeans:

The First Time I Had To Purchase Bigger/Maternity Clothes:

MOMMY TO BE THOUGHTS:

HAVING THE HEART TO LOVE

MOMMY TO BE THOUGHTS: HAVING THE HEART TO LOVE

I Currently Weigh:

I Plan On Having (Natural Birth, Water Birth, Home Birth …):

I Am (Write How Many Weeks):

This Is My (Write If This Is Your First, Second, Or Third Pregnancy):

Pregnancy Makes Me Feel:

I Am Excited About:

I Am Nervous About:

I Am Hoping:

I Never Thought I:

When I Found Out I Was Expecting, I Felt:

MOMMY TO BE THOUGHTS: HAVING THE HEART TO LOVE

The Emotions I Have Been Feeling:

When I Feel Great, It Is Because I Am Thinking:

This Pregnancy Is:

I Have Always Thought:

I Am Expecting:

MOMMY TO BE THOUGHTS: HAVING THE HEART TO LOVE

I Was Always Told:

I Am Prepared To:

I Am Not Prepared To:

I Refuse To:

I Will Stop:

MOMMY TO BE THOUGHTS: HAVING THE HEART TO LOVE

My Support System Includes:

Classes I Plan To Take:

I Believe I Will Be:

I Will Try My Best To:

I Am Worried About:

MOMMY TO BE THOUGHTS: HAVING THE HEART TO LOVE

I Will Pray For:

I Will Keep Track Of:

I Will Learn To:

I Can Get Better At:

I Will Be The Type Of Mom That:

I Will Not Be The Mom That:

I Would Like My Baby Shower To:

I Would Like My Friends And Family To:

It's Not Easy For Me To Admit:

I Think Breastfeeding Is:

MOMMY TO BE THOUGHTS: HAVING THE HEART TO LOVE

I Hope That My Baby:

I Am Experiencing:

I Secretly:

I Feel Like I Am Losing:

I Feel Like I Am Gaining:

MOMMY TO BE THOUGHTS: HAVING THE HEART TO LOVE

I Know It Is Never Too Late To:

My Goals Are:

I Know I Can Still Accomplish:

Some Things I Do Not Want To Change:

Some Things I Have To Change:

MOMMY TO BE THOUGHTS: HAVING THE HEART TO LOVE

I Am Looking Forward To:

When I Found Out I Was Going To Be A Mom:

When I Knew I Was Expecting, The First Baby Name I Thought Of Was:

I Decided To Tell Everyone I Was Pregnant (Write Down When):

Some Things I Still Plan To Do For Me Before The Baby Comes:

MOMMY TO BE THOUGHTS: HAVING THE HEART TO LOVE

Some Things My Partner And I Plan To Do Before The Baby Comes:

My Mommy Style Will Be:

My Current Mom To Be Style Is:

In This New Stage Of Life, I Am:

I Would Love For:

MOMMY TO BE THOUGHTS: HAVING THE HEART TO LOVE

What I'm Going To Miss:

My Morning Sickness Lasted (Answer If Applicable):

THE FIRST FOUR MONTHS:

UNRAVELING
FEELINGS

THE FIRST FOUR MONTHS: UNRAVELING FEELINGS

Date: Mood: Week:

I Feel Like: It Is A Miracle That:

I Am Starting To: Today I Prepared My Mind, Body And
                                          Spirit For A Growing Baby Within Me
                                          By:

I Am Mindful: Today I Prepared For My Baby By:

Today's Mom To Be Workout Was: Today I Did A Good Job:

I Am Getting Use To The Idea:

THE FIRST FOUR MONTHS: UNRAVELING FEELINGS

Date: Mood: Week:

I Feel Like: It Is A Miracle That:

I Am Starting To: Today I Prepared My Mind, Body And
                                              Spirit For A Growing Baby Within Me
                                              By:

I Am Mindful: Today I Prepared For My Baby By:

Today's Mom To Be Workout Was: Today I Did A Good Job:

I Am Getting Use To The Idea:

A LIST OF MY 'OMG' MOMENTS AND THOUGHTS....

THE FIRST FOUR MONTHS: UNRAVELING FEELINGS

Date: Mood: Week:

I Feel Like:

It Is A Miracle That:

I Am Starting To:

Today I Prepared My Mind, Body And Spirit For A Growing Baby Within Me By:

I Am Mindful:

Today I Prepared For My Baby By:

Today's Mom To Be Workout Was:

Today I Did A Good Job:

I Am Getting Use To The Idea:

THE FIRST FOUR MONTHS: UNRAVELING FEELINGS

Date: Mood: Week:

I Feel Like:

It Is A Miracle That:

I Am Starting To:

Today I Prepared My Mind, Body And Spirit For A Growing Baby Within Me By:

I Am Mindful:

Today I Prepared For My Baby By:

Today's Mom To Be Workout Was:

Today I Did A Good Job:

I Am Getting Use To The Idea:

GOD'S TIMING IS PERFECT.

EXCITED. TIRED. CAN'T SLEEP. HAPPY. HUNGRY. PREGNANT.

THE FIRST FOUR MONTHS: UNRAVELING FEELINGS

Date: Mood: Week:

I Feel Like: It Is A Miracle That:

I Am Starting To: Today I Prepared My Mind, Body And
                                         Spirit For A Growing Baby Within Me
                                         By:

I Am Mindful: Today I Prepared For My Baby By:

Today's Mom To Be Workout Was: Today I Did A Good Job:

I Am Getting Use To The Idea:

THE FIRST FOUR MONTHS: UNRAVELING FEELINGS

Date: Mood: Week:

I Feel Like: It Is A Miracle That:

I Am Starting To: Today I Prepared My Mind, Body And
                                     Spirit For A Growing Baby Within Me
                                     By:

I Am Mindful: Today I Prepared For My Baby By:

Today's Mom To Be Workout Was: Today I Did A Good Job:

I Am Getting Use To The Idea:

THE FIRST FOUR MONTHS: UNRAVELING FEELINGS

Date: Mood: Week:

I Feel Like: It Is A Miracle That:

I Am Starting To: Today I Prepared My Mind, Body And
                                      Spirit For A Growing Baby Within Me
                                      By:

I Am Mindful: Today I Prepared For My Baby By:

Today's Mom To Be Workout Was: Today I Did A Good Job:

I Am Getting Use To The Idea:

THE FIRST FOUR MONTHS: UNRAVELING FEELINGS

Date: Mood: Week:

I Feel Like: It Is A Miracle That:

I Am Starting To: Today I Prepared My Mind, Body And
                                          Spirit For A Growing Baby Within Me
                                          By:

I Am Mindful: Today I Prepared For My Baby By:

Today's Mom To Be Workout Was: Today I Did A Good Job:

I Am Getting Use To The Idea:

MOM TO BE THOUGHTS

THE FIRST FOUR MONTHS: UNRAVELING FEELINGS

Date: Mood: Week:

I Feel Like:

It Is A Miracle That:

I Am Starting To:

Today I Prepared My Mind, Body And Spirit For A Growing Baby Within Me By:

I Am Mindful:

Today I Prepared For My Baby By:

Today's Mom To Be Workout Was:

Today I Did A Good Job:

I Am Getting Use To The Idea:

THE FIRST FOUR MONTHS: UNRAVELING FEELINGS

Date: Mood: Week:

I Feel Like:

It Is A Miracle That:

I Am Starting To:

Today I Prepared My Mind, Body And Spirit For A Growing Baby Within Me By:

I Am Mindful:

Today I Prepared For My Baby By:

Today's Mom To Be Workout Was:

Today I Did A Good Job:

I Am Getting Use To The Idea:

A LOVE LETTER TO MY UNBORN CHILD....

THE FIRST FOUR MONTHS: UNRAVELING FEELINGS

Date: Mood: Week:

I Feel Like: It Is A Miracle That:

I Am Starting To: Today I Prepared My Mind, Body And
                                            Spirit For A Growing Baby Within Me
                                            By:

I Am Mindful: Today I Prepared For My Baby By:

Today's Mom To Be Workout Was: Today I Did A Good Job:

I Am Getting Use To The Idea:

THE FIRST FOUR MONTHS: UNRAVELING FEELINGS

Date: Mood: Week:

I Feel Like: It Is A Miracle That:

I Am Starting To: Today I Prepared My Mind, Body And
                                              Spirit For A Growing Baby Within Me
                                              By:

I Am Mindful: Today I Prepared For My Baby By:

Today's Mom To Be Workout Was: Today I Did A Good Job:

I Am Getting Use To The Idea:

THE FIRST FOUR MONTHS: UNRAVELING FEELINGS

Date: Mood: Week:

I Feel Like: It Is A Miracle That:

I Am Starting To: Today I Prepared My Mind, Body And
                                      Spirit For A Growing Baby Within Me
                                      By:

I Am Mindful: Today I Prepared For My Baby By:

Today's Mom To Be Workout Was: Today I Did A Good Job:

I Am Getting Use To The Idea:

I
FEEL
BLESSED.

THE FIRST FOUR MONTHS: UNRAVELING FEELINGS

Date: Mood: Week:

I Feel Like:

It Is A Miracle That:

I Am Starting To:

Today I Prepared My Mind, Body And Spirit For A Growing Baby Within Me By:

I Am Mindful:

Today I Prepared For My Baby By:

Today's Mom To Be Workout Was:

Today I Did A Good Job:

I Am Getting Use To The Idea:

THE FIRST FOUR MONTHS: UNRAVELING FEELINGS

Date: Mood: Week:

I Feel Like: It Is A Miracle That:

I Am Starting To: Today I Prepared My Mind, Body And Spirit For A Growing Baby Within Me By:

I Am Mindful: Today I Prepared For My Baby By:

Today's Mom To Be Workout Was: Today I Did A Good Job:

I Am Getting Use To The Idea:

THE FIRST FOUR MONTHS: UNRAVELING FEELINGS

Date: Mood: Week:

I Feel Like: It Is A Miracle That:

I Am Starting To: Today I Prepared My Mind, Body And
                                      Spirit For A Growing Baby Within Me
                                      By:

I Am Mindful: Today I Prepared For My Baby By:

Today's Mom To Be Workout Was: Today I Did A Good Job:

I Am Getting Use To The Idea:

THE FIRST FOUR MONTHS: UNRAVELING FEELINGS

Date: Mood: Week:

I Feel Like:

It Is A Miracle That:

I Am Starting To:

Today I Prepared My Mind, Body And Spirit For A Growing Baby Within Me By:

I Am Mindful:

Today I Prepared For My Baby By:

Today's Mom To Be Workout Was:

Today I Did A Good Job:

I Am Getting Use To The Idea:

MY HEART IS CONNECTED TO YOURS. I'M ALL IN.

I FEEL BLESSED TO HAVE THIS MIRACLE HAPPEN TO ME.

THE FIRST FOUR MONTHS: UNRAVELING FEELINGS

Date: Mood: Week:

I Feel Like:

It Is A Miracle That:

I Am Starting To:

Today I Prepared My Mind, Body And Spirit For A Growing Baby Within Me By:

I Am Mindful:

Today I Prepared For My Baby By:

Today's Mom To Be Workout Was:

Today I Did A Good Job:

I Am Getting Use To The Idea:

THE FIRST FOUR MONTHS: UNRAVELING FEELINGS

Date: Mood: Week:

I Feel Like: It Is A Miracle That:

I Am Starting To: Today I Prepared My Mind, Body And
                                      Spirit For A Growing Baby Within Me
                                      By:

I Am Mindful: Today I Prepared For My Baby By:

Today's Mom To Be Workout Was: Today I Did A Good Job:

I Am Getting Use To The Idea:

THE FIRST FOUR MONTHS: UNRAVELING FEELINGS

Date: Mood: Week:

I Feel Like:

It Is A Miracle That:

I Am Starting To:

Today I Prepared My Mind, Body And Spirit For A Growing Baby Within Me By:

I Am Mindful:

Today I Prepared For My Baby By:

Today's Mom To Be Workout Was:

Today I Did A Good Job:

I Am Getting Use To The Idea:

MY MOTHER ALWAYS SAID....

THE FIRST FOUR MONTHS: UNRAVELING FEELINGS

Date: Mood: Week:

I Feel Like: It Is A Miracle That:

I Am Starting To: Today I Prepared My Mind, Body And
                                      Spirit For A Growing Baby Within Me
                                      By:

I Am Mindful: Today I Prepared For My Baby By:

Today's Mom To Be Workout Was: Today I Did A Good Job:

I Am Getting Use To The Idea:

THE FIRST FOUR MONTHS: UNRAVELING FEELINGS

Date: Mood: Week:

I Feel Like: It Is A Miracle That:

I Am Starting To: Today I Prepared My Mind, Body And
                                              Spirit For A Growing Baby Within Me
                                              By:

I Am Mindful: Today I Prepared For My Baby By:

Today's Mom To Be Workout Was: Today I Did A Good Job:

I Am Getting Use To The Idea:

THE FIRST FOUR MONTHS: UNRAVELING FEELINGS

Date: Mood: Week:

I Feel Like:

It Is A Miracle That:

I Am Starting To:

Today I Prepared My Mind, Body And Spirit For A Growing Baby Within Me By:

I Am Mindful:

Today I Prepared For My Baby By:

Today's Mom To Be Workout Was:

Today I Did A Good Job:

I Am Getting Use To The Idea:

THE FIRST FOUR MONTHS: UNRAVELING FEELINGS

Date: Mood: Week:

I Feel Like:

It Is A Miracle That:

I Am Starting To:

Today I Prepared My Mind, Body And Spirit For A Growing Baby Within Me By:

I Am Mindful:

Today I Prepared For My Baby By:

Today's Mom To Be Workout Was:

Today I Did A Good Job:

I Am Getting Use To The Idea:

MOM TO BE THOUGHTS

THE FIRST FOUR MONTHS: UNRAVELING FEELINGS

Date: Mood: Week:

I Feel Like: It Is A Miracle That:

I Am Starting To: Today I Prepared My Mind, Body And
                                         Spirit For A Growing Baby Within Me
                                         By:

I Am Mindful: Today I Prepared For My Baby By:

Today's Mom To Be Workout Was: Today I Did A Good Job:

I Am Getting Use To The Idea:

THE FIRST FOUR MONTHS: UNRAVELING FEELINGS

Date: Mood: Week:

I Feel Like: It Is A Miracle That:

I Am Starting To: Today I Prepared My Mind, Body And
                                          Spirit For A Growing Baby Within Me
                                          By:

I Am Mindful: Today I Prepared For My Baby By:

Today's Mom To Be Workout Was: Today I Did A Good Job:

I Am Getting Use To The Idea:

THE FIRST FOUR MONTHS: UNRAVELING FEELINGS

Date: Mood: Week:

I Feel Like:

It Is A Miracle That:

I Am Starting To:

Today I Prepared My Mind, Body And Spirit For A Growing Baby Within Me By:

I Am Mindful:

Today I Prepared For My Baby By:

Today's Mom To Be Workout Was:

Today I Did A Good Job:

I Am Getting Use To The Idea:

MOM TO BE THOUGHTS

I WILL BE THE BEST MOM I CAN BE.

THE FIRST FOUR MONTHS: UNRAVELING FEELINGS

Date: Mood: Week:

I Feel Like: It Is A Miracle That:

I Am Starting To: Today I Prepared My Mind, Body And
                                            Spirit For A Growing Baby Within Me
                                            By:

I Am Mindful: Today I Prepared For My Baby By:

Today's Mom To Be Workout Was: Today I Did A Good Job:

I Am Getting Use To The Idea:

THE FIRST FOUR MONTHS: UNRAVELING FEELINGS

Date: Mood: Week:

I Feel Like:

It Is A Miracle That:

I Am Starting To:

Today I Prepared My Mind, Body And Spirit For A Growing Baby Within Me By:

I Am Mindful:

Today I Prepared For My Baby By:

Today's Mom To Be Workout Was:

Today I Did A Good Job:

I Am Getting Use To The Idea:

THE FIRST FOUR MONTHS: UNRAVELING FEELINGS

Date: Mood: Week:

I Feel Like:

It Is A Miracle That:

I Am Starting To:

Today I Prepared My Mind, Body And Spirit For A Growing Baby Within Me By:

I Am Mindful:

Today I Prepared For My Baby By:

Today's Mom To Be Workout Was:

Today I Did A Good Job:

I Am Getting Use To The Idea:

Date: Mood: Week:

I Feel Like: It Is A Miracle That:

I Am Starting To: Today I Prepared My Mind, Body And
                                         Spirit For A Growing Baby Within Me
                                         By:

I Am Mindful: Today I Prepared For My Baby By:

Today's Mom To Be Workout Was: Today I Did A Good Job:

I Am Getting Use To The Idea:

I WILL MANIFEST A BEAUTIFUL FUTURE FOR YOU THROUGH MY PRAYERS.

NAMES I AM CONSIDERING
IF IT IS A BOY....

NAMES I AM CONSIDERING
IF IT IS A GIRL....

Date: Mood: Week:

I Feel Like: It Is A Miracle That:

I Am Starting To: Today I Prepared My Mind, Body And
                                         Spirit For A Growing Baby Within Me
                                         By:

I Am Mindful: Today I Prepared For My Baby By:

Today's Mom To Be Workout Was: Today I Did A Good Job:

I Am Getting Use To The Idea:

THE FIRST FOUR MONTHS: UNRAVELING FEELINGS

Date: Mood: Week:

I Feel Like:

It Is A Miracle That:

I Am Starting To:

Today I Prepared My Mind, Body And Spirit For A Growing Baby Within Me By:

I Am Mindful:

Today I Prepared For My Baby By:

Today's Mom To Be Workout Was:

Today I Did A Good Job:

I Am Getting Use To The Idea:

THE FIRST FOUR MONTHS: UNRAVELING FEELINGS

Date: Mood: Week:

I Feel Like: It Is A Miracle That:

I Am Starting To: Today I Prepared My Mind, Body And
                                              Spirit For A Growing Baby Within Me
                                              By:

I Am Mindful: Today I Prepared For My Baby By:

Today's Mom To Be Workout Was: Today I Did A Good Job:

I Am Getting Use To The Idea:

I WILL NOT LET MY EMOTIONS GET THE BEST OF ME.

YOU ARE THE RESULT OF LOVE AND PRAYERS.

THE FIRST FOUR MONTHS: UNRAVELING FEELINGS

Date: Mood: Week:

I Feel Like: It Is A Miracle That:

I Am Starting To: Today I Prepared My Mind, Body And
                                            Spirit For A Growing Baby Within Me
                                            By:

I Am Mindful: Today I Prepared For My Baby By:

Today's Mom To Be Workout Was: Today I Did A Good Job:

I Am Getting Use To The Idea:

THE FIRST FOUR MONTHS: UNRAVELING FEELINGS

Date: Mood: Week:

I Feel Like: It Is A Miracle That:

I Am Starting To: Today I Prepared My Mind, Body And
                                         Spirit For A Growing Baby Within Me
                                         By:

I Am Mindful: Today I Prepared For My Baby By:

Today's Mom To Be Workout Was: Today I Did A Good Job:

I Am Getting Use To The Idea:

THE FIRST FOUR MONTHS: UNRAVELING FEELINGS

Date: Mood: Week:

I Feel Like:

It Is A Miracle That:

I Am Starting To:

Today I Prepared My Mind, Body And Spirit For A Growing Baby Within Me By:

I Am Mindful:

Today I Prepared For My Baby By:

Today's Mom To Be Workout Was:

Today I Did A Good Job:

I Am Getting Use To The Idea:

THE FIRST FOUR MONTHS: UNRAVELING FEELINGS

Date: Mood: Week:

I Feel Like: It Is A Miracle That:

I Am Starting To: Today I Prepared My Mind, Body And
                                              Spirit For A Growing Baby Within Me
                                              By:

I Am Mindful: Today I Prepared For My Baby By:

Today's Mom To Be Workout Was: Today I Did A Good Job:

I Am Getting Use To The Idea:

PROMISES I AM MAKING
TO MYSELF....

MOM TO BE THOUGHTS

THE FIRST FOUR MONTHS: UNRAVELING FEELINGS

Date: Mood: Week:

I Feel Like:

It Is A Miracle That:

I Am Starting To:

Today I Prepared My Mind, Body And Spirit For A Growing Baby Within Me By:

I Am Mindful:

Today I Prepared For My Baby By:

Today's Mom To Be Workout Was:

Today I Did A Good Job:

I Am Getting Use To The Idea:

THE FIRST FOUR MONTHS: UNRAVELING FEELINGS

Date: Mood: Week:

I Feel Like:

It Is A Miracle That:

I Am Starting To:

Today I Prepared My Mind, Body And Spirit For A Growing Baby Within Me By:

I Am Mindful:

Today I Prepared For My Baby By:

Today's Mom To Be Workout Was:

Today I Did A Good Job:

I Am Getting Use To The Idea:

THE FIRST FOUR MONTHS: UNRAVELING FEELINGS

Date: Mood: Week:

I Feel Like: It Is A Miracle That:

I Am Starting To: Today I Prepared My Mind, Body And
                                         Spirit For A Growing Baby Within Me
                                         By:

I Am Mindful: Today I Prepared For My Baby By:

Today's Mom To Be Workout Was: Today I Did A Good Job:

I Am Getting Use To The Idea:

IT'S OKAY TO
BE A MOM
AFTER 35, MOM
STUDENT,
AND/OR A MOM
ENTREPRENEUR.

MOM TO BE THOUGHTS

THE FIRST FOUR MONTHS: UNRAVELING FEELINGS

Date: Mood: Week:

I Feel Like:

It Is A Miracle That:

I Am Starting To:

Today I Prepared My Mind, Body And Spirit For A Growing Baby Within Me By:

I Am Mindful:

Today I Prepared For My Baby By:

Today's Mom To Be Workout Was:

Today I Did A Good Job:

I Am Getting Use To The Idea:

THE FIRST FOUR MONTHS: UNRAVELING FEELINGS

Date: Mood: Week:

I Feel Like:

It Is A Miracle That:

I Am Starting To:

Today I Prepared My Mind, Body And Spirit For A Growing Baby Within Me By:

I Am Mindful:

Today I Prepared For My Baby By:

Today's Mom To Be Workout Was:

Today I Did A Good Job:

I Am Getting Use To The Idea:

A LETTER TO MY FUTURE MOMMY SELF....

MOM TO BE THOUGHTS

THE FIRST FOUR MONTHS: UNRAVELING FEELINGS

Date: Mood: Week:

I Feel Like:

It Is A Miracle That:

I Am Starting To:

Today I Prepared My Mind, Body And Spirit For A Growing Baby Within Me By:

I Am Mindful:

Today I Prepared For My Baby By:

Today's Mom To Be Workout Was:

Today I Did A Good Job:

I Am Getting Use To The Idea:

THE FIRST FOUR MONTHS: UNRAVELING FEELINGS

Date: Mood: Week:

I Feel Like: It Is A Miracle That:

I Am Starting To: Today I Prepared My Mind, Body And
                                     Spirit For A Growing Baby Within Me
                                     By:

I Am Mindful: Today I Prepared For My Baby By:

Today's Mom To Be Workout Was: Today I Did A Good Job:

I Am Getting Use To The Idea:

THE FIRST FOUR MONTHS: UNRAVELING FEELINGS

Date: Mood: Week:

I Feel Like: It Is A Miracle That:

I Am Starting To: Today I Prepared My Mind, Body And
                                              Spirit For A Growing Baby Within Me
                                              By:

I Am Mindful: Today I Prepared For My Baby By:

Today's Mom To Be Workout Was: Today I Did A Good Job:

I Am Getting Use To The Idea:

THE FIRST FOUR MONTHS: UNRAVELING FEELINGS

Date: Mood: Week:

I Feel Like:

It Is A Miracle That:

I Am Starting To:

Today I Prepared My Mind, Body And Spirit For A Growing Baby Within Me By:

I Am Mindful:

Today I Prepared For My Baby By:

Today's Mom To Be Workout Was:

Today I Did A Good Job:

I Am Getting Use To The Idea:

THE FIRST FOUR MONTHS: UNRAVELING FEELINGS

Date: Mood: Week:

I Feel Like: It Is A Miracle That:

I Am Starting To: Today I Prepared My Mind, Body And
                                            Spirit For A Growing Baby Within Me
                                            By:

I Am Mindful: Today I Prepared For My Baby By:

Today's Mom To Be Workout Was: Today I Did A Good Job:

I Am Getting Use To The Idea:

MY PREGNANCY INSPIRES ME TO BE MY BEST.

THEY SAY
SURROUND
YOURSELF
WITH OTHER
MOMS. I THINK
I'LL JUST
SURROUND
MYSELF WITH
FOOD.

THE FIRST FOUR MONTHS: UNRAVELING FEELINGS

Date: Mood: Week:

I Feel Like: It Is A Miracle That:

I Am Starting To: Today I Prepared My Mind, Body And
                                      Spirit For A Growing Baby Within Me
                                      By:

I Am Mindful: Today I Prepared For My Baby By:

Today's Mom To Be Workout Was: Today I Did A Good Job:

I Am Getting Use To The Idea:

THE FIRST FOUR MONTHS: UNRAVELING FEELINGS

Date: Mood: Week:

I Feel Like: It Is A Miracle That:

I Am Starting To: Today I Prepared My Mind, Body And
                                                 Spirit For A Growing Baby Within Me
                                                 By:

I Am Mindful: Today I Prepared For My Baby By:

Today's Mom To Be Workout Was: Today I Did A Good Job:

I Am Getting Use To The Idea:

THE FIRST FOUR MONTHS: UNRAVELING FEELINGS

Date: Mood: Week:

I Feel Like:

It Is A Miracle That:

I Am Starting To:

Today I Prepared My Mind, Body And Spirit For A Growing Baby Within Me By:

I Am Mindful:

Today I Prepared For My Baby By:

Today's Mom To Be Workout Was:

Today I Did A Good Job:

I Am Getting Use To The Idea:

BABYMOON IDEAS....

Date: Mood: Week:

I Feel Like: It Is A Miracle That:

I Am Starting To: Today I Prepared My Mind, Body And
                                            Spirit For A Growing Baby Within Me
                                            By:

I Am Mindful: Today I Prepared For My Baby By:

Today's Mom To Be Workout Was: Today I Did A Good Job:

I Am Getting Use To The Idea:

THE FIRST FOUR MONTHS: UNRAVELING FEELINGS

Date: Mood: Week:

I Feel Like: It Is A Miracle That:

I Am Starting To: Today I Prepared My Mind, Body And
                                      Spirit For A Growing Baby Within Me
                                      By:

I Am Mindful: Today I Prepared For My Baby By:

Today's Mom To Be Workout Was: Today I Did A Good Job:

I Am Getting Use To The Idea:

I FEEL BEAUTIFUL TODAY.

THE FIRST FOUR MONTHS: UNRAVELING FEELINGS

Date: Mood: Week:

I Feel Like:

It Is A Miracle That:

I Am Starting To:

Today I Prepared My Mind, Body And Spirit For A Growing Baby Within Me By:

I Am Mindful:

Today I Prepared For My Baby By:

Today's Mom To Be Workout Was:

Today I Did A Good Job:

I Am Getting Use To The Idea:

THE FIRST FOUR MONTHS: UNRAVELING FEELINGS

Date: Mood: Week:

I Feel Like: It Is A Miracle That:

I Am Starting To: Today I Prepared My Mind, Body And
                                       Spirit For A Growing Baby Within Me
                                       By:

I Am Mindful: Today I Prepared For My Baby By:

Today's Mom To Be Workout Was: Today I Did A Good Job:

I Am Getting Use To The Idea:

HAVING YOU IS ME HAVING EVERYTHING.

I WILL REACH MY GOALS WITH YOU.

THE FIRST FOUR MONTHS: UNRAVELING FEELINGS

Date: Mood: Week:

I Feel Like: It Is A Miracle That:

I Am Starting To: Today I Prepared My Mind, Body And
                                               Spirit For A Growing Baby Within Me
                                               By:

I Am Mindful: Today I Prepared For My Baby By:

Today's Mom To Be Workout Was: Today I Did A Good Job:

I Am Getting Use To The Idea:

THE FIRST FOUR MONTHS: UNRAVELING FEELINGS

Date: Mood: Week:

I Feel Like:

It Is A Miracle That:

I Am Starting To:

Today I Prepared My Mind, Body And Spirit For A Growing Baby Within Me By:

I Am Mindful:

Today I Prepared For My Baby By:

Today's Mom To Be Workout Was:

Today I Did A Good Job:

I Am Getting Use To The Idea:

THE FIRST FOUR MONTHS: UNRAVELING FEELINGS

Date: Mood: Week:

I Feel Like: It Is A Miracle That:

I Am Starting To: Today I Prepared My Mind, Body And
                                            Spirit For A Growing Baby Within Me
                                            By:

I Am Mindful: Today I Prepared For My Baby By:

Today's Mom To Be Workout Was: Today I Did A Good Job:

I Am Getting Use To The Idea:

THE FIRST FOUR MONTHS: UNRAVELING FEELINGS

Date: Mood: Week:

I Feel Like:

It Is A Miracle That:

I Am Starting To:

Today I Prepared My Mind, Body And Spirit For A Growing Baby Within Me By:

I Am Mindful:

Today I Prepared For My Baby By:

Today's Mom To Be Workout Was:

Today I Did A Good Job:

I Am Getting Use To The Idea:

THE FIRST FOUR MONTHS: UNRAVELING FEELINGS

Date: Mood: Week:

I Feel Like:

It Is A Miracle That:

I Am Starting To:

Today I Prepared My Mind, Body And Spirit For A Growing Baby Within Me By:

I Am Mindful:

Today I Prepared For My Baby By:

Today's Mom To Be Workout Was:

Today I Did A Good Job:

I Am Getting Use To The Idea:

THE FIRST FOUR MONTHS: UNRAVELING FEELINGS

Date: Mood: Week:

I Feel Like:

It Is A Miracle That:

I Am Starting To:

Today I Prepared My Mind, Body And Spirit For A Growing Baby Within Me By:

I Am Mindful:

Today I Prepared For My Baby By:

Today's Mom To Be Workout Was:

Today I Did A Good Job:

I Am Getting Use To The Idea:

EVEN AS A MOM, I WILL CONTINUE TO....

GOD GAVE ME YOU, THEREFORE THIS ISN'T A MISTAKE.

THE FIRST FOUR MONTHS: UNRAVELING FEELINGS

Date: Mood: Week:

I Feel Like:

It Is A Miracle That:

I Am Starting To:

Today I Prepared My Mind, Body And Spirit For A Growing Baby Within Me By:

I Am Mindful:

Today I Prepared For My Baby By:

Today's Mom To Be Workout Was:

Today I Did A Good Job:

I Am Getting Use To The Idea:

THE FIRST FOUR MONTHS: UNRAVELING FEELINGS

Date: Mood: Week:

I Feel Like:

It Is A Miracle That:

I Am Starting To:

Today I Prepared My Mind, Body And Spirit For A Growing Baby Within Me By:

I Am Mindful:

Today I Prepared For My Baby By:

Today's Mom To Be Workout Was:

Today I Did A Good Job:

I Am Getting Use To The Idea:

I CURRENTLY FEEL
LOVED WHEN....

I AM READY TO RECEIVE YOU AS MY MIRACLE.

THE FIRST FOUR MONTHS: UNRAVELING FEELINGS

Date: Mood: Week:

I Feel Like: It Is A Miracle That:

I Am Starting To: Today I Prepared My Mind, Body And
                                               Spirit For A Growing Baby Within Me
                                               By:

I Am Mindful: Today I Prepared For My Baby By:

Today's Mom To Be Workout Was: Today I Did A Good Job:

I Am Getting Use To The Idea:

THE FIRST FOUR MONTHS: UNRAVELING FEELINGS

Date: Mood: Week:

I Feel Like: It Is A Miracle That:

I Am Starting To: Today I Prepared My Mind, Body And
                                         Spirit For A Growing Baby Within Me
                                         By:

I Am Mindful: Today I Prepared For My Baby By:

Today's Mom To Be Workout Was: Today I Did A Good Job:

I Am Getting Use To The Idea:

THE FIRST FOUR MONTHS: UNRAVELING FEELINGS

Date: Mood: Week:

I Feel Like: It Is A Miracle That:

I Am Starting To: Today I Prepared My Mind, Body And
                                            Spirit For A Growing Baby Within Me
                                            By:

I Am Mindful: Today I Prepared For My Baby By:

Today's Mom To Be Workout Was: Today I Did A Good Job:

I Am Getting Use To The Idea:

THE FIRST FOUR MONTHS: UNRAVELING FEELINGS

Date: Mood: Week:

I Feel Like: It Is A Miracle That:

I Am Starting To: Today I Prepared My Mind, Body And
                                          Spirit For A Growing Baby Within Me
                                          By:

I Am Mindful: Today I Prepared For My Baby By:

Today's Mom To Be Workout Was: Today I Did A Good Job:

I Am Getting Use To The Idea:

THE FIRST FOUR MONTHS: UNRAVELING FEELINGS

Date: Mood: Week:

I Feel Like: It Is A Miracle That:

I Am Starting To: Today I Prepared My Mind, Body And
                                          Spirit For A Growing Baby Within Me
                                          By:

I Am Mindful: Today I Prepared For My Baby By:

Today's Mom To Be Workout Was: Today I Did A Good Job:

I Am Getting Use To The Idea:

WHEN I GIVE, IT WON'T COME WITH STRINGS. I GIVE BECAUSE I LOVE YOU.

THANK YOU GOD FOR YOUR LOVE.

THE FIRST FOUR MONTHS: UNRAVELING FEELINGS

Date: Mood: Week:

I Feel Like: It Is A Miracle That:

I Am Starting To: Today I Prepared My Mind, Body And
                                                       Spirit For A Growing Baby Within Me
                                                       By:

I Am Mindful: Today I Prepared For My Baby By:

Today's Mom To Be Workout Was: Today I Did A Good Job:

I Am Getting Use To The Idea:

THE FIRST FOUR MONTHS: UNRAVELING FEELINGS

Date: Mood: Week:

I Feel Like:

It Is A Miracle That:

I Am Starting To:

Today I Prepared My Mind, Body And Spirit For A Growing Baby Within Me By:

I Am Mindful:

Today I Prepared For My Baby By:

Today's Mom To Be Workout Was:

Today I Did A Good Job:

I Am Getting Use To The Idea:

THE FIRST FOUR MONTHS: UNRAVELING FEELINGS

Date: Mood: Week:

I Feel Like: It Is A Miracle That:

I Am Starting To: Today I Prepared My Mind, Body And
                                          Spirit For A Growing Baby Within Me
                                          By:

I Am Mindful: Today I Prepared For My Baby By:

Today's Mom To Be Workout Was: Today I Did A Good Job:

I Am Getting Use To The Idea:

MY MIND IS ALWAYS ON....

THE FIRST FOUR MONTHS: UNRAVELING FEELINGS

Date: Mood: Week:

I Feel Like:

It Is A Miracle That:

I Am Starting To:

Today I Prepared My Mind, Body And Spirit For A Growing Baby Within Me By:

I Am Mindful:

Today I Prepared For My Baby By:

Today's Mom To Be Workout Was:

Today I Did A Good Job:

I Am Getting Use To The Idea:

THE FIRST FOUR MONTHS: UNRAVELING FEELINGS

Date: Mood: Week:

I Feel Like:

It Is A Miracle That:

I Am Starting To:

Today I Prepared My Mind, Body And Spirit For A Growing Baby Within Me By:

I Am Mindful:

Today I Prepared For My Baby By:

Today's Mom To Be Workout Was:

Today I Did A Good Job:

I Am Getting Use To The Idea:

THE FIRST FOUR MONTHS: UNRAVELING FEELINGS

Date: Mood: Week:

I Feel Like: It Is A Miracle That:

I Am Starting To: Today I Prepared My Mind, Body And
                                                  Spirit For A Growing Baby Within Me
                                                  By:

I Am Mindful: Today I Prepared For My Baby By:

Today's Mom To Be Workout Was: Today I Did A Good Job:

I Am Getting Use To The Idea:

THE BEST THING ABOUT
BEING PREGNANT....

LOVING YOU IS LOVING GOD AND EVERYTHING HE IS.

I'LL NEVER STOP WORKING ON ME BECAUSE OF YOU.

Date: Mood: Week:

I Feel Like: It Is A Miracle That:

I Am Starting To: Today I Prepared My Mind, Body And
                                         Spirit For A Growing Baby Within Me
                                         By:

I Am Mindful: Today I Prepared For My Baby By:

Today's Mom To Be Workout Was: Today I Did A Good Job:

I Am Getting Use To The Idea:

Date: Mood: Week:

I Feel Like: It Is A Miracle That:

I Am Starting To: Today I Prepared My Mind, Body And
                                                Spirit For A Growing Baby Within Me
                                                By:

I Am Mindful: Today I Prepared For My Baby By:

Today's Mom To Be Workout Was: Today I Did A Good Job:

I Am Getting Use To The Idea:

THE FIRST FOUR MONTHS: UNRAVELING FEELINGS

Date: Mood: Week:

I Feel Like: It Is A Miracle That:

I Am Starting To: Today I Prepared My Mind, Body And
                                          Spirit For A Growing Baby Within Me
                                          By:

I Am Mindful: Today I Prepared For My Baby By:

Today's Mom To Be Workout Was: Today I Did A Good Job:

I Am Getting Use To The Idea:

THE FIRST FOUR MONTHS: UNRAVELING FEELINGS

Date: Mood: Week:

I Feel Like:

It Is A Miracle That:

I Am Starting To:

Today I Prepared My Mind, Body And Spirit For A Growing Baby Within Me By:

I Am Mindful:

Today I Prepared For My Baby By:

Today's Mom To Be Workout Was:

Today I Did A Good Job:

I Am Getting Use To The Idea:

MY PROMISE TO YOU....
TO LOVE, PROTECT, & TEACH.

I AM GROWING AN ANGEL INSIDE OF ME.

THE FIRST FOUR MONTHS: UNRAVELING FEELINGS

Date: Mood: Week:

I Feel Like: It Is A Miracle That:

I Am Starting To: Today I Prepared My Mind, Body And
                                                Spirit For A Growing Baby Within Me
                                                By:

I Am Mindful: Today I Prepared For My Baby By:

Today's Mom To Be Workout Was: Today I Did A Good Job:

I Am Getting Use To The Idea:

THE FIRST FOUR MONTHS: UNRAVELING FEELINGS

Date: Mood: Week:

I Feel Like:

It Is A Miracle That:

I Am Starting To:

Today I Prepared My Mind, Body And Spirit For A Growing Baby Within Me By:

I Am Mindful:

Today I Prepared For My Baby By:

Today's Mom To Be Workout Was:

Today I Did A Good Job:

I Am Getting Use To The Idea:

THE FIRST FOUR MONTHS: UNRAVELING FEELINGS

Date: Mood: Week:

I Feel Like:

It Is A Miracle That:

I Am Starting To:

Today I Prepared My Mind, Body And Spirit For A Growing Baby Within Me By:

I Am Mindful:

Today I Prepared For My Baby By:

Today's Mom To Be Workout Was:

Today I Did A Good Job:

I Am Getting Use To The Idea:

I AM MAKING ROOM FOR MY BABY BY....

THE FIRST FOUR MONTHS: UNRAVELING FEELINGS

Date: Mood: Week:

I Feel Like:

It Is A Miracle That:

I Am Starting To:

Today I Prepared My Mind, Body And Spirit For A Growing Baby Within Me By:

I Am Mindful:

Today I Prepared For My Baby By:

Today's Mom To Be Workout Was:

Today I Did A Good Job:

I Am Getting Use To The Idea:

THE FIRST FOUR MONTHS: UNRAVELING FEELINGS

Date: Mood: Week:

I Feel Like:

It Is A Miracle That:

I Am Starting To:

Today I Prepared My Mind, Body And Spirit For A Growing Baby Within Me By:

I Am Mindful:

Today I Prepared For My Baby By:

Today's Mom To Be Workout Was:

Today I Did A Good Job:

I Am Getting Use To The Idea:

IS IT OKAY IF I LOVE YOU MORE TODAY THAN I DID YESTERDAY?

THE FIRST FOUR MONTHS: UNRAVELING FEELINGS

Date: Mood: Week:

I Feel Like: It Is A Miracle That:

I Am Starting To: Today I Prepared My Mind, Body And
                                                Spirit For A Growing Baby Within Me
                                                By:

I Am Mindful: Today I Prepared For My Baby By:

Today's Mom To Be Workout Was: Today I Did A Good Job:

I Am Getting Use To The Idea:

THE FIRST FOUR MONTHS: UNRAVELING FEELINGS

Date: Mood: Week:

I Feel Like: It Is A Miracle That:

I Am Starting To: Today I Prepared My Mind, Body And
                                            Spirit For A Growing Baby Within Me
                                            By:

I Am Mindful: Today I Prepared For My Baby By:

Today's Mom To Be Workout Was: Today I Did A Good Job:

I Am Getting Use To The Idea:

YOU WERE ALWAYS A PART OF GOD'S PLAN.

MOM TO BE THOUGHTS

THE FIRST FOUR MONTHS: UNRAVELING FEELINGS

Date: Mood: Week:

I Feel Like: It Is A Miracle That:

I Am Starting To: Today I Prepared My Mind, Body And
                                                Spirit For A Growing Baby Within Me
                                                By:

I Am Mindful: Today I Prepared For My Baby By:

Today's Mom To Be Workout Was: Today I Did A Good Job:

I Am Getting Use To The Idea:

THE FIRST FOUR MONTHS: UNRAVELING FEELINGS

Date: Mood: Week:

I Feel Like: It Is A Miracle That:

I Am Starting To: Today I Prepared My Mind, Body And
                                      Spirit For A Growing Baby Within Me
                                      By:

I Am Mindful: Today I Prepared For My Baby By:

Today's Mom To Be Workout Was: Today I Did A Good Job:

I Am Getting Use To The Idea:

MOM TO BE THOUGHTS

THE FIRST FOUR MONTHS: UNRAVELING FEELINGS

Date: Mood: Week:

I Feel Like: It Is A Miracle That:

I Am Starting To: Today I Prepared My Mind, Body And
                                          Spirit For A Growing Baby Within Me
                                          By:

I Am Mindful: Today I Prepared For My Baby By:

Today's Mom To Be Workout Was: Today I Did A Good Job:

I Am Getting Use To The Idea:

THE FIRST FOUR MONTHS: UNRAVELING FEELINGS

Date: Mood: Week:

I Feel Like: It Is A Miracle That:

I Am Starting To: Today I Prepared My Mind, Body And
                                                  Spirit For A Growing Baby Within Me
                                                  By:

I Am Mindful: Today I Prepared For My Baby By:

Today's Mom To Be Workout Was: Today I Did A Good Job:

I Am Getting Use To The Idea:

THE FIRST FOUR MONTHS: UNRAVELING FEELINGS

Date: Mood: Week:

I Feel Like: It Is A Miracle That:

I Am Starting To: Today I Prepared My Mind, Body And
                                          Spirit For A Growing Baby Within Me
                                          By:

I Am Mindful: Today I Prepared For My Baby By:

Today's Mom To Be Workout Was: Today I Did A Good Job:

I Am Getting Use To The Idea:

FIVE PLACES I GO TO CLEAR MY MIND....

1.

2.

3.

4.

5.

MOMMY TO BE THOUGHTS:

PERMISSION TO STAND IN MY TRUTH

MOMMY TO BE THOUGHTS:
PERMISSION TO STAND IN MY TRUTH

I Feel Guilty About:

I Expected:

I Am Enjoying:

I Started Seeing Stretch Marks:

The Things I Have Been Doing For Myself:

MOMMY TO BE THOUGHTS:
PERMISSION TO STAND IN MY TRUTH

I Decided To Not Go Overboard On:

I Have Changed My Mind On:

Tasks I Now Delagate To My Partner Or Someone Else:

What I Am Keeping To Myself:

I Stopped Trying:

MOMMY TO BE THOUGHTS:
PERMISSION TO STAND IN MY TRUTH

I Started Trying:

I Want To Be Known As:

I Want To Finish:

Planning For My Baby Requires:

I Am Giving Myself Time To:

MOMMY TO BE THOUGHTS:
PERMISSION TO STAND IN MY TRUTH

I Congratulate Myself For:

I Underestimated:

I Am Happy That I Am Still Able To:

I Can Only Hope These Next Few Months Are:

No One Ever Tells You:

Once In A While I Think:

Everyone Says:

I've Been Dreaming:

Some Nights I:

Some Of The Weird Things I Find Myself Doing:

MOMMY TO BE THOUGHTS:
PERMISSION TO STAND IN MY TRUTH

My Friendships Are:

I Like That:

I Dislike:

I Am Falling In Love With:

I Remember This Time Last Year, I Was:

MOMMY TO BE THOUGHTS:
PERMISSION TO STAND IN MY TRUTH

I've Been So Worried With:

Financially, I Am:

The Things I Have Left To Do:

Surprisingly, I Am:

A Few Things That Have Happened To Me That Had Me Going Through
A Roller Coaster Of Emotions:

MOMMY TO BE THOUGHTS:
PERMISSION TO STAND IN MY TRUTH

I Am Not Just A Mom To Be, I Am A:

My Pregnancy Is Going:

What I Love About My Pregnancy:

What I Dislike About My Pregnancy:

I Find Myself Being More:

MOMMY TO BE THOUGHTS:
PERMISSION TO STAND IN MY TRUTH

I Find Myself Being Less:

I Calm Myself Down By:

For Our Babymoon, We Are Going (Answer If Applicable):

The Advice I Have Been Getting About Maintaining My Body:

The Best Advice I Have Gotten About Being A New Mom:

MOMMY TO BE THOUGHTS:
PERMISSION TO STAND IN MY TRUTH

I No Longer Want To Hear About:

It Annoys Me When:

I Spend My Free Time:

I Am Happy To Feel:

I Am Still Very Private About:

MOMMY TO BE THOUGHTS: PERMISSION TO STAND IN MY TRUTH

I Have Learned That:

This Pregnancy Has Taught Me:

The Parts Of Me That I Feel Have Gotten Better:

I Am Now Concerned With:

THE CHANGES:
LOVING MYSELF
THROUGH IT

THE CHANGES: LOVING MYSELF THROUGH IT

Date: Mood: Week:

Today I Want To Thank: Parts Of My Body That Hurt And/Or
                                          Feel Uncomfortable:

Today I Want To Tell My Baby: Foods I Am Eating More/Less Of:

What I Am Loving About This   I Feel Like My Baby Will Bring Me
Pregnancy: Closer To:

Changes I Am Feeling: Everyday I Thank God For:

Changes I Am Noticing:

THE CHANGES: LOVING MYSELF THROUGH IT

Date: Mood: Week:

Today I Want To Thank: Parts Of My Body That Hurt And/Or
                                    Feel Uncomfortable:

Today I Want To Tell My Baby: Foods I Am Eating More/Less Of:

What I Am Loving About This   I Feel Like My Baby Will Bring Me
Pregnancy: Closer To:

Changes I Am Feeling: Everyday I Thank God For:

Changes I Am Noticing:

THE CHANGES: LOVING MYSELF THROUGH IT

Date: Mood: Week:

Today I Want To Thank: Parts Of My Body That Hurt And/Or
                                          Feel Uncomfortable:

Today I Want To Tell My Baby: Foods I Am Eating More/Less Of:

What I Am Loving About This   I Feel Like My Baby Will Bring Me
Pregnancy: Closer To:

Changes I Am Feeling: Everyday I Thank God For:

Changes I Am Noticing:

MOM TO BE THOUGHTS

MY LOVE FOR YOU KEEPS GROWING STRONGER AND STRONGER DAY BY DAY.

THE CHANGES: LOVING MYSELF THROUGH IT

Date: Mood: Week:

Today I Want To Thank: Parts Of My Body That Hurt And/Or
                                    Feel Uncomfortable:

Today I Want To Tell My Baby: Foods I Am Eating More/Less Of:

What I Am Loving About This   I Feel Like My Baby Will Bring Me
Pregnancy: Closer To:

Changes I Am Feeling: Everyday I Thank God For:

Changes I Am Noticing:

THE CHANGES: LOVING MYSELF THROUGH IT

Date: Mood: Week:

Today I Want To Thank: Parts Of My Body That Hurt And/Or
                                    Feel Uncomfortable:

Today I Want To Tell My Baby: Foods I Am Eating More/Less Of:

What I Am Loving About This   I Feel Like My Baby Will Bring Me
Pregnancy: Closer To:

Changes I Am Feeling: Everyday I Thank God For:

Changes I Am Noticing:

THE CHANGES: LOVING MYSELF THROUGH IT

Date: Mood: Week:

Today I Want To Thank: Parts Of My Body That Hurt And/Or
                                          Feel Uncomfortable:

Today I Want To Tell My Baby: Foods I Am Eating More/Less Of:

What I Am Loving About This   I Feel Like My Baby Will Bring Me
Pregnancy: Closer To:

Changes I Am Feeling: Everyday I Thank God For:

Changes I Am Noticing:

THE CHANGES: LOVING MYSELF THROUGH IT

Date: Mood: Week:

Today I Want To Thank: Parts Of My Body That Hurt And/Or
                                                Feel Uncomfortable:

Today I Want To Tell My Baby: Foods I Am Eating More/Less Of:

What I Am Loving About This   I Feel Like My Baby Will Bring Me
Pregnancy: Closer To:

Changes I Am Feeling: Everyday I Thank God For:

Changes I Am Noticing:

I'M TIRED RIGHT NOW, BUT GUESS WHAT...A BLESSING IS ON THE WAY.

TODAY WASN'T ONE OF MY BEST DAYS, BUT IT WAS STILL A BLESSING BECAUSE WE SPENT IT TOGETHER.

MOM TO BE THOUGHTS

MY BODY FEELS LIKE UGH, BUT MY BABY BUMP IS OVERFLOWING WITH LOVE.

THE CHANGES: LOVING MYSELF THROUGH IT

Date: Mood: Week:

Today I Want To Thank:

Parts Of My Body That Hurt And/Or Feel Uncomfortable:

Today I Want To Tell My Baby:

Foods I Am Eating More/Less Of:

What I Am Loving About This Pregnancy:

I Feel Like My Baby Will Bring Me Closer To:

Changes I Am Feeling:

Everyday I Thank God For:

Changes I Am Noticing:

THE CHANGES: LOVING MYSELF THROUGH IT

Date: Mood: Week:

Today I Want To Thank: Parts Of My Body That Hurt And/Or
                                          Feel Uncomfortable:

Today I Want To Tell My Baby: Foods I Am Eating More/Less Of:

What I Am Loving About This   I Feel Like My Baby Will Bring Me
Pregnancy: Closer To:

Changes I Am Feeling: Everyday I Thank God For:

Changes I Am Noticing:

THE CHANGES: LOVING MYSELF THROUGH IT

Date: Mood: Week:

Today I Want To Thank: Parts Of My Body That Hurt And/Or Feel Uncomfortable:

Today I Want To Tell My Baby: Foods I Am Eating More/Less Of:

What I Am Loving About This Pregnancy: I Feel Like My Baby Will Bring Me Closer To:

Changes I Am Feeling: Everyday I Thank God For:

Changes I Am Noticing:

BOOKS I'VE BEEN READING....

AN UNEXPECTED NINE MONTHS IS AN UNEXPECTED BLESSING.

THE CHANGES: LOVING MYSELF THROUGH IT

Date: Mood: Week:

Today I Want To Thank:

Parts Of My Body That Hurt And/Or Feel Uncomfortable:

Today I Want To Tell My Baby:

Foods I Am Eating More/Less Of:

What I Am Loving About This Pregnancy:

I Feel Like My Baby Will Bring Me Closer To:

Changes I Am Feeling:

Everyday I Thank God For:

Changes I Am Noticing:

THE CHANGES: LOVING MYSELF THROUGH IT

Date: Mood: Week:

Today I Want To Thank: Parts Of My Body That Hurt And/Or
                                          Feel Uncomfortable:

Today I Want To Tell My Baby: Foods I Am Eating More/Less Of:

What I Am Loving About This   I Feel Like My Baby Will Bring Me
Pregnancy: Closer To:

Changes I Am Feeling: Everyday I Thank God For:

Changes I Am Noticing:

THE CHANGES: LOVING MYSELF THROUGH IT

Date: Mood: Week:

Today I Want To Thank: Parts Of My Body That Hurt And/Or
                                          Feel Uncomfortable:

Today I Want To Tell My Baby: Foods I Am Eating More/Less Of:

What I Am Loving About This   I Feel Like My Baby Will Bring Me
Pregnancy: Closer To:

Changes I Am Feeling: Everyday I Thank God For:

Changes I Am Noticing:

DESPITE MY BODY CHANGING, MY BEAUTY IS STILL THE SAME.

THE CHANGES: LOVING MYSELF THROUGH IT

Date: Mood: Week:

Today I Want To Thank: Parts Of My Body That Hurt And/Or
                                          Feel Uncomfortable:

Today I Want To Tell My Baby: Foods I Am Eating More/Less Of:

What I Am Loving About This   I Feel Like My Baby Will Bring Me
Pregnancy: Closer To:

Changes I Am Feeling: Everyday I Thank God For:

Changes I Am Noticing:

THE CHANGES: LOVING MYSELF THROUGH IT

Date: Mood: Week:

Today I Want To Thank: Parts Of My Body That Hurt And/Or
                                          Feel Uncomfortable:

Today I Want To Tell My Baby: Foods I Am Eating More/Less Of:

What I Am Loving About This   I Feel Like My Baby Will Bring Me
Pregnancy: Closer To:

Changes I Am Feeling: Everyday I Thank God For:

Changes I Am Noticing:

MOM TO BE THOUGHTS

THE CHANGES: LOVING MYSELF THROUGH IT

Date: Mood: Week:

Today I Want To Thank: Parts Of My Body That Hurt And/Or
                                          Feel Uncomfortable:

Today I Want To Tell My Baby: Foods I Am Eating More/Less Of:

What I Am Loving About This   I Feel Like My Baby Will Bring Me
Pregnancy: Closer To:

Changes I Am Feeling: Everyday I Thank God For:

Changes I Am Noticing:

THE CHANGES: LOVING MYSELF THROUGH IT

Date: Mood: Week:

Today I Want To Thank: Parts Of My Body That Hurt And/Or
                                    Feel Uncomfortable:

Today I Want To Tell My Baby: Foods I Am Eating More/Less Of:

What I Am Loving About This   I Feel Like My Baby Will Bring Me
Pregnancy: Closer To:

Changes I Am Feeling: Everyday I Thank God For:

Changes I Am Noticing:

THE CHANGES: LOVING MYSELF THROUGH IT

Date: Mood: Week:

Today I Want To Thank: Parts Of My Body That Hurt And/Or
                                          Feel Uncomfortable:

Today I Want To Tell My Baby: Foods I Am Eating More/Less Of:

What I Am Loving About This   I Feel Like My Baby Will Bring Me
Pregnancy: Closer To:

Changes I Am Feeling: Everyday I Thank God For:

Changes I Am Noticing:

MOM TO BE THOUGHTS

THE CHANGES: LOVING MYSELF THROUGH IT

Date: Mood: Week:

Today I Want To Thank: Parts Of My Body That Hurt And/Or
                                          Feel Uncomfortable:

Today I Want To Tell My Baby: Foods I Am Eating More/Less Of:

What I Am Loving About This   I Feel Like My Baby Will Bring Me
Pregnancy: Closer To:

Changes I Am Feeling: Everyday I Thank God For:

Changes I Am Noticing:

THE CHANGES: LOVING MYSELF THROUGH IT

Date: Mood: Week:

Today I Want To Thank: Parts Of My Body That Hurt And/Or
                                        Feel Uncomfortable:

Today I Want To Tell My Baby: Foods I Am Eating More/Less Of:

What I Am Loving About This   I Feel Like My Baby Will Bring Me
Pregnancy: Closer To:

Changes I Am Feeling: Everyday I Thank God For:

Changes I Am Noticing:

THE CHANGES: LOVING MYSELF THROUGH IT

Date: Mood: Week:

Today I Want To Thank:

Parts Of My Body That Hurt And/Or Feel Uncomfortable:

Today I Want To Tell My Baby:

Foods I Am Eating More/Less Of:

What I Am Loving About This Pregnancy:

I Feel Like My Baby Will Bring Me Closer To:

Changes I Am Feeling:

Everyday I Thank God For:

Changes I Am Noticing:

THE CHANGES: LOVING MYSELF THROUGH IT

Date: Mood: Week:

Today I Want To Thank:

Parts Of My Body That Hurt And/Or Feel Uncomfortable:

Today I Want To Tell My Baby:

Foods I Am Eating More/Less Of:

What I Am Loving About This Pregnancy:

I Feel Like My Baby Will Bring Me Closer To:

Changes I Am Feeling:

Everyday I Thank God For:

Changes I Am Noticing:

FIVE THINGS I WANT TO REMEMBER AS I PREPARE TO BECOME A MOTHER....

1.

2.

3.

4.

5.

I AM A CONFIDENT QUEEN REGARDLESS OF WHAT THESE NEXT FEW MONTHS BRING IN.

MY BABY BUMP IS BIG BECAUSE OF THE LOVE.

THE CHANGES: LOVING MYSELF THROUGH IT

Date: Mood: Week:

Today I Want To Thank: Parts Of My Body That Hurt And/Or
                                            Feel Uncomfortable:

Today I Want To Tell My Baby: Foods I Am Eating More/Less Of:

What I Am Loving About This   I Feel Like My Baby Will Bring Me
Pregnancy: Closer To:

Changes I Am Feeling: Everyday I Thank God For:

Changes I Am Noticing:

THE CHANGES: LOVING MYSELF THROUGH IT

Date: Mood: Week:

Today I Want To Thank: Parts Of My Body That Hurt And/Or
                                    Feel Uncomfortable:

Today I Want To Tell My Baby: Foods I Am Eating More/Less Of:

What I Am Loving About This   I Feel Like My Baby Will Bring Me
Pregnancy: Closer To:

Changes I Am Feeling: Everyday I Thank God For:

Changes I Am Noticing:

THE CHANGES: LOVING MYSELF THROUGH IT

Date: Mood: Week:

Today I Want To Thank: Parts Of My Body That Hurt And/Or
                                          Feel Uncomfortable:

Today I Want To Tell My Baby: Foods I Am Eating More/Less Of:

What I Am Loving About This   I Feel Like My Baby Will Bring Me
Pregnancy: Closer To:

Changes I Am Feeling: Everyday I Thank God For:

Changes I Am Noticing:

THE CHANGES: LOVING MYSELF THROUGH IT

Date: Mood: Week:

Today I Want To Thank: Parts Of My Body That Hurt And/Or
                                      Feel Uncomfortable:

Today I Want To Tell My Baby: Foods I Am Eating More/Less Of:

What I Am Loving About This   I Feel Like My Baby Will Bring Me
Pregnancy: Closer To:

Changes I Am Feeling: Everyday I Thank God For:

Changes I Am Noticing:

WAIT TO MEET MY NEW BEST FRIEND.

MOM TO BE THOUGHTS

THE CHANGES: LOVING MYSELF THROUGH IT

Date: Mood: Week:

Today I Want To Thank:

Parts Of My Body That Hurt And/Or Feel Uncomfortable:

Today I Want To Tell My Baby:

Foods I Am Eating More/Less Of:

What I Am Loving About This Pregnancy:

I Feel Like My Baby Will Bring Me Closer To:

Changes I Am Feeling:

Everyday I Thank God For:

Changes I Am Noticing:

THE CHANGES: LOVING MYSELF THROUGH IT

Date: Mood: Week:

Today I Want To Thank: Parts Of My Body That Hurt And/Or
                                     Feel Uncomfortable:

Today I Want To Tell My Baby: Foods I Am Eating More/Less Of:

What I Am Loving About This   I Feel Like My Baby Will Bring Me
Pregnancy: Closer To:

Changes I Am Feeling: Everyday I Thank God For:

Changes I Am Noticing:

THE CHANGES: LOVING MYSELF THROUGH IT

Date: Mood: Week:

Today I Want To Thank: Parts Of My Body That Hurt And/Or
                                          Feel Uncomfortable:

Today I Want To Tell My Baby: Foods I Am Eating More/Less Of:

What I Am Loving About This   I Feel Like My Baby Will Bring Me
Pregnancy: Closer To:

Changes I Am Feeling: Everyday I Thank God For:

Changes I Am Noticing:

THINGS I WOULD LIKE TO GET DONE BEFORE MY BABY ARRIVES....

THE CHANGES: LOVING MYSELF THROUGH IT

Date: Mood: Week:

Today I Want To Thank: Parts Of My Body That Hurt And/Or
                                          Feel Uncomfortable:

Today I Want To Tell My Baby: Foods I Am Eating More/Less Of:

What I Am Loving About This   I Feel Like My Baby Will Bring Me
Pregnancy: Closer To:

Changes I Am Feeling: Everyday I Thank God For:

Changes I Am Noticing:

THE CHANGES: LOVING MYSELF THROUGH IT

Date: Mood: Week:

Today I Want To Thank:

Parts Of My Body That Hurt And/Or Feel Uncomfortable:

Today I Want To Tell My Baby:

Foods I Am Eating More/Less Of:

What I Am Loving About This Pregnancy:

I Feel Like My Baby Will Bring Me Closer To:

Changes I Am Feeling:

Everyday I Thank God For:

Changes I Am Noticing:

THE CHANGES: LOVING MYSELF THROUGH IT

Date: Mood: Week:

Today I Want To Thank: Parts Of My Body That Hurt And/Or
                                          Feel Uncomfortable:

Today I Want To Tell My Baby: Foods I Am Eating More/Less Of:

What I Am Loving About This   I Feel Like My Baby Will Bring Me
Pregnancy: Closer To:

Changes I Am Feeling: Everyday I Thank God For:

Changes I Am Noticing:

UNDERSTANDING THAT MY PREGNANCY EXPERIENCE IS DIFFERENT.

MOM TO BE THOUGHTS

THE CHANGES: LOVING MYSELF THROUGH IT

Date: Mood: Week:

Today I Want To Thank: Parts Of My Body That Hurt And/Or
                                          Feel Uncomfortable:

Today I Want To Tell My Baby: Foods I Am Eating More/Less Of:

What I Am Loving About This   I Feel Like My Baby Will Bring Me
Pregnancy: Closer To:

Changes I Am Feeling: Everyday I Thank God For:

Changes I Am Noticing:

THE CHANGES: LOVING MYSELF THROUGH IT

Date: Mood: Week:

Today I Want To Thank:

Parts Of My Body That Hurt And/Or Feel Uncomfortable:

Today I Want To Tell My Baby:

Foods I Am Eating More/Less Of:

What I Am Loving About This Pregnancy:

I Feel Like My Baby Will Bring Me Closer To:

Changes I Am Feeling:

Everyday I Thank God For:

Changes I Am Noticing:

I ALWAYS KNEW THAT THERE WAS A BEAUTIFUL LIFE INSIDE OF ME.

THE CHANGES: LOVING MYSELF THROUGH IT

Date: Mood: Week:

Today I Want To Thank:

Parts Of My Body That Hurt And/Or Feel Uncomfortable:

Today I Want To Tell My Baby:

Foods I Am Eating More/Less Of:

What I Am Loving About This Pregnancy:

I Feel Like My Baby Will Bring Me Closer To:

Changes I Am Feeling:

Everyday I Thank God For:

Changes I Am Noticing:

MOM TO BE THOUGHTS

THE CHANGES: LOVING MYSELF THROUGH IT

Date: Mood: Week:

Today I Want To Thank: Parts Of My Body That Hurt And/Or
                                          Feel Uncomfortable:

Today I Want To Tell My Baby: Foods I Am Eating More/Less Of:

What I Am Loving About This   I Feel Like My Baby Will Bring Me
Pregnancy: Closer To:

Changes I Am Feeling: Everyday I Thank God For:

Changes I Am Noticing:

THE CHANGES: LOVING MYSELF THROUGH IT

Date: Mood: Week:

Today I Want To Thank: Parts Of My Body That Hurt And/Or
                                    Feel Uncomfortable:

Today I Want To Tell My Baby: Foods I Am Eating More/Less Of:

What I Am Loving About This   I Feel Like My Baby Will Bring Me
Pregnancy: Closer To:

Changes I Am Feeling: Everyday I Thank God For:

Changes I Am Noticing:

THE CHANGES: LOVING MYSELF THROUGH IT

Date: Mood: Week:

Today I Want To Thank: Parts Of My Body That Hurt And/Or
                                          Feel Uncomfortable:

Today I Want To Tell My Baby: Foods I Am Eating More/Less Of:

What I Am Loving About This   I Feel Like My Baby Will Bring Me
Pregnancy: Closer To:

Changes I Am Feeling: Everyday I Thank God For:

Changes I Am Noticing:

THE SAME LOVE THAT MADE YOU, IS THE SAME LOVE THAT WILL HELP YOU TO GROW.

THE CHANGES: LOVING MYSELF THROUGH IT

Date: Mood: Week:

Today I Want To Thank: Parts Of My Body That Hurt And/Or
                                          Feel Uncomfortable:

Today I Want To Tell My Baby: Foods I Am Eating More/Less Of:

What I Am Loving About This   I Feel Like My Baby Will Bring Me
Pregnancy: Closer To:

Changes I Am Feeling: Everyday I Thank God For:

Changes I Am Noticing:

SOME GIFTS I REALLY HOPE I GET....

THE CHANGES: LOVING MYSELF THROUGH IT

Date: Mood: Week:

Today I Want To Thank: Parts Of My Body That Hurt And/Or
                                         Feel Uncomfortable:

Today I Want To Tell My Baby: Foods I Am Eating More/Less Of:

What I Am Loving About This   I Feel Like My Baby Will Bring Me
Pregnancy: Closer To:

Changes I Am Feeling: Everyday I Thank God For:

Changes I Am Noticing:

THE CHANGES: LOVING MYSELF THROUGH IT

Date: Mood: Week:

Today I Want To Thank: | Parts Of My Body That Hurt And/Or Feel Uncomfortable:

Today I Want To Tell My Baby: | Foods I Am Eating More/Less Of:

What I Am Loving About This Pregnancy: | I Feel Like My Baby Will Bring Me Closer To:

Changes I Am Feeling: | Everyday I Thank God For:

Changes I Am Noticing:

THE CHANGES: LOVING MYSELF THROUGH IT

Date: Mood: Week:

Today I Want To Thank: | Parts Of My Body That Hurt And/Or Feel Uncomfortable:

Today I Want To Tell My Baby: | Foods I Am Eating More/Less Of:

What I Am Loving About This Pregnancy: | I Feel Like My Baby Will Bring Me Closer To:

Changes I Am Feeling: | Everyday I Thank God For:

Changes I Am Noticing:

THE CHANGES: LOVING MYSELF THROUGH IT

Date: Mood: Week:

Today I Want To Thank:

Parts Of My Body That Hurt And/Or Feel Uncomfortable:

Today I Want To Tell My Baby:

Foods I Am Eating More/Less Of:

What I Am Loving About This Pregnancy:

I Feel Like My Baby Will Bring Me Closer To:

Changes I Am Feeling:

Everyday I Thank God For:

Changes I Am Noticing:

MOM TO BE THOUGHTS

I KNOW I AM CAPABLE OF LOVING YOU AS GOD INTENDED.

THE CHANGES: LOVING MYSELF THROUGH IT

Date: Mood: Week:

Today I Want To Thank: Parts Of My Body That Hurt And/Or
                                          Feel Uncomfortable:

Today I Want To Tell My Baby: Foods I Am Eating More/Less Of:

What I Am Loving About This   I Feel Like My Baby Will Bring Me
Pregnancy: Closer To:

Changes I Am Feeling: Everyday I Thank God For:

Changes I Am Noticing:

THE CHANGES: LOVING MYSELF THROUGH IT

Date: Mood: Week:

Today I Want To Thank: Parts Of My Body That Hurt And/Or
                                     Feel Uncomfortable:

Today I Want To Tell My Baby: Foods I Am Eating More/Less Of:

What I Am Loving About This   I Feel Like My Baby Will Bring Me
Pregnancy: Closer To:

Changes I Am Feeling: Everyday I Thank God For:

Changes I Am Noticing:

THE CHANGES: LOVING MYSELF THROUGH IT

Date: Mood: Week:

Today I Want To Thank: Parts Of My Body That Hurt And/Or
                                       Feel Uncomfortable:

Today I Want To Tell My Baby: Foods I Am Eating More/Less Of:

What I Am Loving About This   I Feel Like My Baby Will Bring Me
Pregnancy: Closer To:

Changes I Am Feeling: Everyday I Thank God For:

Changes I Am Noticing:

I'M ALWAYS TELLING
MY BABY....

THE CHANGES: LOVING MYSELF THROUGH IT

Date: Mood: Week:

Today I Want To Thank:

Parts Of My Body That Hurt And/Or
Feel Uncomfortable:

Today I Want To Tell My Baby:

Foods I Am Eating More/Less Of:

What I Am Loving About This
Pregnancy:

I Feel Like My Baby Will Bring Me
Closer To:

Changes I Am Feeling:

Everyday I Thank God For:

Changes I Am Noticing:

THE CHANGES: LOVING MYSELF THROUGH IT

Date: Mood: Week:

Today I Want To Thank: Parts Of My Body That Hurt And/Or
                                          Feel Uncomfortable:

Today I Want To Tell My Baby: Foods I Am Eating More/Less Of:

What I Am Loving About This   I Feel Like My Baby Will Bring Me
Pregnancy: Closer To:

Changes I Am Feeling: Everyday I Thank God For:

Changes I Am Noticing:

THE CHANGES: LOVING MYSELF THROUGH IT

Date: Mood: Week:

Today I Want To Thank: | Parts Of My Body That Hurt And/Or Feel Uncomfortable:

Today I Want To Tell My Baby: | Foods I Am Eating More/Less Of:

What I Am Loving About This Pregnancy: | I Feel Like My Baby Will Bring Me Closer To:

Changes I Am Feeling: | Everyday I Thank God For:

Changes I Am Noticing:

MOM TO BE THOUGHTS

THE CHANGES: LOVING MYSELF THROUGH IT

Date: Mood: Week:

Today I Want To Thank: Parts Of My Body That Hurt And/Or
                                          Feel Uncomfortable:

Today I Want To Tell My Baby: Foods I Am Eating More/Less Of:

What I Am Loving About This   I Feel Like My Baby Will Bring Me
Pregnancy: Closer To:

Changes I Am Feeling: Everyday I Thank God For:

Changes I Am Noticing:

THE CHANGES: LOVING MYSELF THROUGH IT

Date: Mood: Week:

Today I Want To Thank:

Parts Of My Body That Hurt And/Or Feel Uncomfortable:

Today I Want To Tell My Baby:

Foods I Am Eating More/Less Of:

What I Am Loving About This Pregnancy:

I Feel Like My Baby Will Bring Me Closer To:

Changes I Am Feeling:

Everyday I Thank God For:

Changes I Am Noticing:

THE CHANGES: LOVING MYSELF THROUGH IT

Date: Mood: Week:

Today I Want To Thank: Parts Of My Body That Hurt And/Or
                                          Feel Uncomfortable:

Today I Want To Tell My Baby: Foods I Am Eating More/Less Of:

What I Am Loving About This   I Feel Like My Baby Will Bring Me
Pregnancy: Closer To:

Changes I Am Feeling: Everyday I Thank God For:

Changes I Am Noticing:

I BELIEVE I WILL LOOK BACK AT THIS TIME OF MY LIFE AND SAY....

THE CHANGES: LOVING MYSELF THROUGH IT

Date: Mood: Week:

Today I Want To Thank:

Parts Of My Body That Hurt And/Or Feel Uncomfortable:

Today I Want To Tell My Baby:

Foods I Am Eating More/Less Of:

What I Am Loving About This Pregnancy:

I Feel Like My Baby Will Bring Me Closer To:

Changes I Am Feeling:

Everyday I Thank God For:

Changes I Am Noticing:

MOM TO BE THOUGHTS

WATCH OUT WORLD!!! THERE IS A MINI ME COMING IN A FEW MONTHS.

THE CHANGES: LOVING MYSELF THROUGH IT

Date: Mood: Week:

Today I Want To Thank: Parts Of My Body That Hurt And/Or
                                  Feel Uncomfortable:

Today I Want To Tell My Baby: Foods I Am Eating More/Less Of:

What I Am Loving About This   I Feel Like My Baby Will Bring Me
Pregnancy: Closer To:

Changes I Am Feeling: Everyday I Thank God For:

Changes I Am Noticing:

THE CHANGES: LOVING MYSELF THROUGH IT

Date: Mood: Week:

Today I Want To Thank:

Parts Of My Body That Hurt And/Or Feel Uncomfortable:

Today I Want To Tell My Baby:

Foods I Am Eating More/Less Of:

What I Am Loving About This Pregnancy:

I Feel Like My Baby Will Bring Me Closer To:

Changes I Am Feeling:

Everyday I Thank God For:

Changes I Am Noticing:

THE CHANGES: LOVING MYSELF THROUGH IT

Date: Mood: Week:

Today I Want To Thank: Parts Of My Body That Hurt And/Or
                                        Feel Uncomfortable:

Today I Want To Tell My Baby: Foods I Am Eating More/Less Of:

What I Am Loving About This   I Feel Like My Baby Will Bring Me
Pregnancy: Closer To:

Changes I Am Feeling: Everyday I Thank God For:

Changes I Am Noticing:

BECAUSE OF THIS PREGNANCY, I HAVE EXPERIENCED....

GAINING YOU DOESN'T MEAN LOSING ME.

THE CHANGES: LOVING MYSELF THROUGH IT

Date: Mood: Week:

Today I Want To Thank:

Parts Of My Body That Hurt And/Or Feel Uncomfortable:

Today I Want To Tell My Baby:

Foods I Am Eating More/Less Of:

What I Am Loving About This Pregnancy:

I Feel Like My Baby Will Bring Me Closer To:

Changes I Am Feeling:

Everyday I Thank God For:

Changes I Am Noticing:

THE CHANGES: LOVING MYSELF THROUGH IT

Date: Mood: Week:

Today I Want To Thank: Parts Of My Body That Hurt And/Or
                                          Feel Uncomfortable:

Today I Want To Tell My Baby: Foods I Am Eating More/Less Of:

What I Am Loving About This   I Feel Like My Baby Will Bring Me
Pregnancy: Closer To:

Changes I Am Feeling: Everyday I Thank God For:

Changes I Am Noticing:

THE CHANGES: LOVING MYSELF THROUGH IT

Date: Mood: Week:

Today I Want To Thank: Parts Of My Body That Hurt And/Or
                                          Feel Uncomfortable:

Today I Want To Tell My Baby: Foods I Am Eating More/Less Of:

What I Am Loving About This   I Feel Like My Baby Will Bring Me
Pregnancy: Closer To:

Changes I Am Feeling: Everyday I Thank God For:

Changes I Am Noticing:

THE CHANGES: LOVING MYSELF THROUGH IT

Date: Mood: Week:

Today I Want To Thank: | Parts Of My Body That Hurt And/Or Feel Uncomfortable:

Today I Want To Tell My Baby: | Foods I Am Eating More/Less Of:

What I Am Loving About This Pregnancy: | I Feel Like My Baby Will Bring Me Closer To:

Changes I Am Feeling: | Everyday I Thank God For:

Changes I Am Noticing:

MOM TO BE THOUGHTS

THE CHANGES: LOVING MYSELF THROUGH IT

Date: Mood: Week:

Today I Want To Thank: Parts Of My Body That Hurt And/Or
                                    Feel Uncomfortable:

Today I Want To Tell My Baby: Foods I Am Eating More/Less Of:

What I Am Loving About This   I Feel Like My Baby Will Bring Me
Pregnancy: Closer To:

Changes I Am Feeling: Everyday I Thank God For:

Changes I Am Noticing:

THE CHANGES: LOVING MYSELF THROUGH IT

Date: Mood: Week:

Today I Want To Thank: Parts Of My Body That Hurt And/Or
                                          Feel Uncomfortable:

Today I Want To Tell My Baby: Foods I Am Eating More/Less Of:

What I Am Loving About This   I Feel Like My Baby Will Bring Me
Pregnancy: Closer To:

Changes I Am Feeling: Everyday I Thank God For:

Changes I Am Noticing:

THE CHANGES: LOVING MYSELF THROUGH IT

Date: Mood: Week:

Today I Want To Thank: Parts Of My Body That Hurt And/Or
                                          Feel Uncomfortable:

Today I Want To Tell My Baby: Foods I Am Eating More/Less Of:

What I Am Loving About This   I Feel Like My Baby Will Bring Me
Pregnancy: Closer To:

Changes I Am Feeling: Everyday I Thank God For:

Changes I Am Noticing:

YOU'RE ONLY MAKING ME BETTER.

THE CHANGES: LOVING MYSELF THROUGH IT

Date: Mood: Week:

Today I Want To Thank:

Parts Of My Body That Hurt And/Or Feel Uncomfortable:

Today I Want To Tell My Baby:

Foods I Am Eating More/Less Of:

What I Am Loving About This Pregnancy:

I Feel Like My Baby Will Bring Me Closer To:

Changes I Am Feeling:

Everyday I Thank God For:

Changes I Am Noticing:

THE CHANGES: LOVING MYSELF THROUGH IT

Date: Mood: Week:

Today I Want To Thank: Parts Of My Body That Hurt And/Or
                                          Feel Uncomfortable:

Today I Want To Tell My Baby: Foods I Am Eating More/Less Of:

What I Am Loving About This   I Feel Like My Baby Will Bring Me
Pregnancy: Closer To:

Changes I Am Feeling: Everyday I Thank God For:

Changes I Am Noticing:

THE CHANGES: LOVING MYSELF THROUGH IT

Date: Mood: Week:

Today I Want To Thank: Parts Of My Body That Hurt And/Or
                                          Feel Uncomfortable:

Today I Want To Tell My Baby: Foods I Am Eating More/Less Of:

What I Am Loving About This   I Feel Like My Baby Will Bring Me
Pregnancy: Closer To:

Changes I Am Feeling: Everyday I Thank God For:

Changes I Am Noticing:

SOME COMPLICATIONS I HAVE BEEN EXPERIENCING....

MOM TO BE THOUGHTS

THE CHANGES: LOVING MYSELF THROUGH IT

Date: Mood: Week:

Today I Want To Thank:

Parts Of My Body That Hurt And/Or Feel Uncomfortable:

Today I Want To Tell My Baby:

Foods I Am Eating More/Less Of:

What I Am Loving About This Pregnancy:

I Feel Like My Baby Will Bring Me Closer To:

Changes I Am Feeling:

Everyday I Thank God For:

Changes I Am Noticing:

THE CHANGES: LOVING MYSELF THROUGH IT

Date: Mood: Week:

Today I Want To Thank: Parts Of My Body That Hurt And/Or
                                          Feel Uncomfortable:

Today I Want To Tell My Baby: Foods I Am Eating More/Less Of:

What I Am Loving About This   I Feel Like My Baby Will Bring Me
Pregnancy: Closer To:

Changes I Am Feeling: Everyday I Thank God For:

Changes I Am Noticing:

THE CHANGES: LOVING MYSELF THROUGH IT

Date: Mood: Week:

Today I Want To Thank:

Parts Of My Body That Hurt And/Or Feel Uncomfortable:

Today I Want To Tell My Baby:

Foods I Am Eating More/Less Of:

What I Am Loving About This Pregnancy:

I Feel Like My Baby Will Bring Me Closer To:

Changes I Am Feeling:

Everyday I Thank God For:

Changes I Am Noticing:

I KNOW THIS WON'T BE EASY, BUT LOVING YOU WILL BE WORTH IT.

THE CHANGES: LOVING MYSELF THROUGH IT

Date: Mood: Week:

Today I Want To Thank: | Parts Of My Body That Hurt And/Or Feel Uncomfortable:

Today I Want To Tell My Baby: | Foods I Am Eating More/Less Of:

What I Am Loving About This Pregnancy: | I Feel Like My Baby Will Bring Me Closer To:

Changes I Am Feeling: | Everyday I Thank God For:

Changes I Am Noticing:

THE CHANGES: LOVING MYSELF THROUGH IT

Date: Mood: Week:

Today I Want To Thank:

Parts Of My Body That Hurt And/Or Feel Uncomfortable:

Today I Want To Tell My Baby:

Foods I Am Eating More/Less Of:

What I Am Loving About This Pregnancy:

I Feel Like My Baby Will Bring Me Closer To:

Changes I Am Feeling:

Everyday I Thank God For:

Changes I Am Noticing:

YOU'RE THE ONLY GIFT I NEED.

THE CHANGES: LOVING MYSELF THROUGH IT

Date: Mood: Week:

Today I Want To Thank: Parts Of My Body That Hurt And/Or
                                          Feel Uncomfortable:

Today I Want To Tell My Baby: Foods I Am Eating More/Less Of:

What I Am Loving About This   I Feel Like My Baby Will Bring Me
Pregnancy: Closer To:

Changes I Am Feeling: Everyday I Thank God For:

Changes I Am Noticing:

THE CHANGES: LOVING MYSELF THROUGH IT

Date: Mood: Week:

Today I Want To Thank: Parts Of My Body That Hurt And/Or
                                          Feel Uncomfortable:

Today I Want To Tell My Baby: Foods I Am Eating More/Less Of:

What I Am Loving About This   I Feel Like My Baby Will Bring Me
Pregnancy: Closer To:

Changes I Am Feeling: Everyday I Thank God For:

Changes I Am Noticing:

287

MOM TO BE THOUGHTS

CURRENTLY, MY DAILY ROUTINE CONSISTS OF....

THE CHANGES: LOVING MYSELF THROUGH IT

Date: Mood: Week:

Today I Want To Thank: Parts Of My Body That Hurt And/Or
                                         Feel Uncomfortable:

Today I Want To Tell My Baby: Foods I Am Eating More/Less Of:

What I Am Loving About This   I Feel Like My Baby Will Bring Me
Pregnancy: Closer To:

Changes I Am Feeling: Everyday I Thank God For:

Changes I Am Noticing:

THE CHANGES: LOVING MYSELF THROUGH IT

Date: Mood: Week:

Today I Want To Thank:

Parts Of My Body That Hurt And/Or Feel Uncomfortable:

Today I Want To Tell My Baby:

Foods I Am Eating More/Less Of:

What I Am Loving About This Pregnancy:

I Feel Like My Baby Will Bring Me Closer To:

Changes I Am Feeling:

Everyday I Thank God For:

Changes I Am Noticing:

THE CHANGES: LOVING MYSELF THROUGH IT

Date: Mood: Week:

Today I Want To Thank: Parts Of My Body That Hurt And/Or
                                        Feel Uncomfortable:

Today I Want To Tell My Baby: Foods I Am Eating More/Less Of:

What I Am Loving About This   I Feel Like My Baby Will Bring Me
Pregnancy: Closer To:

Changes I Am Feeling: Everyday I Thank God For:

Changes I Am Noticing:

THANK YOU FOR REQUIRING ME TO GROW UP.

THE CHANGES: LOVING MYSELF THROUGH IT

Date: Mood: Week:

Today I Want To Thank: Parts Of My Body That Hurt And/Or
                                          Feel Uncomfortable:

Today I Want To Tell My Baby: Foods I Am Eating More/Less Of:

What I Am Loving About This   I Feel Like My Baby Will Bring Me
Pregnancy: Closer To:

Changes I Am Feeling: Everyday I Thank God For:

Changes I Am Noticing:

THE CHANGES: LOVING MYSELF THROUGH IT

Date: Mood: Week:

Today I Want To Thank: Parts Of My Body That Hurt And/Or
                                          Feel Uncomfortable:

Today I Want To Tell My Baby: Foods I Am Eating More/Less Of:

What I Am Loving About This   I Feel Like My Baby Will Bring Me
Pregnancy: Closer To:

Changes I Am Feeling: Everyday I Thank God For:

Changes I Am Noticing:

THE CHANGES: LOVING MYSELF THROUGH IT

Date: Mood: Week:

Today I Want To Thank:

Parts Of My Body That Hurt And/Or Feel Uncomfortable:

Today I Want To Tell My Baby:

Foods I Am Eating More/Less Of:

What I Am Loving About This Pregnancy:

I Feel Like My Baby Will Bring Me Closer To:

Changes I Am Feeling:

Everyday I Thank God For:

Changes I Am Noticing:

MOM TO BE THOUGHTS

THE CHANGES: LOVING MYSELF THROUGH IT

Date: Mood: Week:

Today I Want To Thank:

Parts Of My Body That Hurt And/Or Feel Uncomfortable:

Today I Want To Tell My Baby:

Foods I Am Eating More/Less Of:

What I Am Loving About This Pregnancy:

I Feel Like My Baby Will Bring Me Closer To:

Changes I Am Feeling:

Everyday I Thank God For:

Changes I Am Noticing:

THE CHANGES: LOVING MYSELF THROUGH IT

Date: Mood: Week:

Today I Want To Thank: Parts Of My Body That Hurt And/Or
                                          Feel Uncomfortable:

Today I Want To Tell My Baby: Foods I Am Eating More/Less Of:

What I Am Loving About This   I Feel Like My Baby Will Bring Me
Pregnancy: Closer To:

Changes I Am Feeling: Everyday I Thank God For:

Changes I Am Noticing:

AS EVERYDAY PASSES, I GET MORE AND MORE EXCITED TO MEET YOU.

THE CHANGES: LOVING MYSELF THROUGH IT

Date: Mood: Week:

Today I Want To Thank: Parts Of My Body That Hurt And/Or
                                                Feel Uncomfortable:

Today I Want To Tell My Baby: Foods I Am Eating More/Less Of:

What I Am Loving About This   I Feel Like My Baby Will Bring Me
Pregnancy: Closer To:

Changes I Am Feeling: Everyday I Thank God For:

Changes I Am Noticing:

THE CHANGES: LOVING MYSELF THROUGH IT

Date: Mood: Week:

Today I Want To Thank: Parts Of My Body That Hurt And/Or
                                      Feel Uncomfortable:

Today I Want To Tell My Baby: Foods I Am Eating More/Less Of:

What I Am Loving About This   I Feel Like My Baby Will Bring Me
Pregnancy: Closer To:

Changes I Am Feeling: Everyday I Thank God For:

Changes I Am Noticing:

THE CHANGES: LOVING MYSELF THROUGH IT

Date: Mood: Week:

Today I Want To Thank: Parts Of My Body That Hurt And/Or
                                          Feel Uncomfortable:

Today I Want To Tell My Baby: Foods I Am Eating More/Less Of:

What I Am Loving About This   I Feel Like My Baby Will Bring Me
Pregnancy: Closer To:

Changes I Am Feeling: Everyday I Thank God For:

Changes I Am Noticing:

5 SONGS THAT MAKE ME FEEL GOOD....

1.

2.

3.

4.

5.

MOM TO BE THOUGHTS

THE CHANGES: LOVING MYSELF THROUGH IT

Date: Mood: Week:

Today I Want To Thank: Parts Of My Body That Hurt And/Or
                                          Feel Uncomfortable:

Today I Want To Tell My Baby: Foods I Am Eating More/Less Of:

What I Am Loving About This   I Feel Like My Baby Will Bring Me
Pregnancy: Closer To:

Changes I Am Feeling: Everyday I Thank God For:

Changes I Am Noticing:

THE CHANGES: LOVING MYSELF THROUGH IT

Date: Mood: Week:

Today I Want To Thank: Parts Of My Body That Hurt And/Or
                                          Feel Uncomfortable:

Today I Want To Tell My Baby: Foods I Am Eating More/Less Of:

What I Am Loving About This   I Feel Like My Baby Will Bring Me
Pregnancy: Closer To:

Changes I Am Feeling: Everyday I Thank God For:

Changes I Am Noticing:

SEX FEELS LIKE....

MOM TO BE THOUGHTS

THE CHANGES: LOVING MYSELF THROUGH IT

Date: Mood: Week:

Today I Want To Thank:

Parts Of My Body That Hurt And/Or Feel Uncomfortable:

Today I Want To Tell My Baby:

Foods I Am Eating More/Less Of:

What I Am Loving About This Pregnancy:

I Feel Like My Baby Will Bring Me Closer To:

Changes I Am Feeling:

Everyday I Thank God For:

Changes I Am Noticing:

I'M NOT AFRAID OF LOVING EVERYTHING GOOD THAT COMES INTO MY LIFE. THIS INCLUDES YOU.

Made in the USA
Columbia, SC
08 November 2022

70585475R00170